Coming Together Around
What Matters Most

A Six-Week Devotional Journey

What Are We Fighting For?
Coming Together Around
What Matters Most

What Are We Fighting For?
Coming Together Around What Matters Most
978-1-5018-1505-8
978-1-5018-1506-5 eBook

What Are We Fighting For? Leader Guide
978-1-5018-1507-2
978-1-5018-1508-9 eBook

What Are We Fighting For? DVD
9781501815119

Coming Together Around What Matters Most:
A Six-Week Devotional Journey
978-1-5018-1509-6
978-1-5018-1510-2 eBook

What Are We Fighting For? Pastor Resources Download
978-1-5018-1513-3

For more information, visit www.AbingdonPress.com.

Thomas J. Bickerton

COMING TOGETHER AROUND
WHAT MATTERS MOST

A SIX-WEEK
DEVOTIONAL JOURNEY

Abingdon Press / Nashville

Coming Together Around What Matters Most:
A Six-Week Devotional Journey

Library of Congress Cataloging-in-Publication applied for.

Names: Bickerton, Thomas J., author. | Bickerton, Thomas J. What are we fighting for?

Title: Coming together around what matters most : a six-week devotional journey / Thomas J. Bickerton.

Description: First [edition]. | Nashville, Tennessee : Abingdon Press, 2016. | Excerpts from: Author's What are we fighting for? with devotional material added.

Identifiers: LCCN 2016005654 | ISBN 9781501815096 (papberback)

Subjects: LCSH: Mission of the church--Prayers and devotions. | Church--Unity--Prayers and devotions. | Methodist Church--Doctrines--Prayers and devotions.

Classification: LCC BV601.8 .B5338 2016 | DDC 287/.6--dc23 LC record available at http://lccn.loc.gov/2016005654

16 17 18 19 20 21 22 23 24 25 — 10 9 8 7 6 5 4 3 2 1
MANUFACTURED IN THE UNITED STATES OF AMERICA

To my parents,
Jim and Marlene Bickerton,
the best storytellers and supporters I know.

CONTENTS

INTRODUCTION

Trying to figure out what matters most—in our personal lives and in our churches—is hard work. It requires patience, focus, and intentionality. In order to be able to rely on instinct and spontaneity, we must discipline ourselves to be in the right posture to receive God's guidance and direction. Actors rehearse their lines and set the stage in order to carry out the play. Athletes warm up and study their playbooks in anticipation of the big game. Scientists work on formulas and carry out experiments in the hopes of making a new discovery. It's all about preparation, anticipation, and a clearly desired outcome. In the same way, we must exercise care and discipline if we are to "set the stage" for determining what matters most.

This book provides a six-week devotional journey for determining what matters most. Each week begins with an excerpt from *What Are We Fighting For? Coming Together Around What Matters Most*, followed by five days of devotional readings. Each devotion invites you to take time to read, reflect, and pray, inviting God to show you how you can become a better reflection of Christ in your daily walk. As you read, prayerfully open yourself to the indwelling of God's Holy Spirit within you. With the inspiration of the Spirit, let these words soften you where you are hard, fill you where you are empty, energize you where you are weak, spark you where the embers have grown cold, and bless you with revelations of what matters most.

A common table prayer often recited before a meal simply says:

> Come, Lord Jesus, be our guest.
> And let these gifts to us be blest.

Come, Lord Jesus, be our guest. Invite Jesus into your discernment of what matters most. Invite Christ into your heart and into the rhythm of your daily life. Invite Christ into the life of your church—your worship services, committee meetings, and strategy sessions. Invite him into whatever void or uncertainty you may have.

And let these gifts to us be blest. What God provides just might disrupt your preconceived notions or the routine of your life. When the gifts of God come, initially they may not seem like blessings if there are significant changes that need to take place within you—or within your church. The prayer simply asks that we allow God to bless us. This will require us to be willing to let God take us as we are and craft us into beings who are eager for and receptive of God's blessings.

This is how we prepare ourselves for the revelation of what God intends for us and for the church. As you faithfully embark on the discovery of the essentials for your life and the ministry of your church, may this simple prayer and these devotions be the salt and light that will provide the seasoning and exposure necessary in order to come together around what matters most.

May it be so! Amen.

Thomas J. Bickerton

Week One

GETTING TO THE HEART OF THE MATTER

I pray that you may have the power to comprehend, with all the saints, what is the breadth and length and height and depth, and to know the love of Christ that surpasses knowledge, so that you may be filled with all the fullness of God.

Now to him who by the power at work within us is able to accomplish abundantly far more than all we can ask or imagine, to him be glory in the church and in Christ Jesus to all generations, forever and ever. Amen.

(Ephesians 3:18-21)

S piritual problems require intensive doses of prayer, study, reflection, and conversation in order to find the renewal that is needed and desired. Spiritual problems require confession and a willingness to be wrong.... I believe that at the heart of all the issues we are debating as a church is a spiritual problem.

Though it is tempting to seek instant answers to complex problems, it is important for us to begin at the heart of the matter and work our way to discover carefully discerned answers to complex issues. Information in the twenty-first century may be just a Google search away, but the renewal and revival of the church will require much more intentionality if we are to determine what we are fighting for while avoiding the temptation to fight for things that are peripheral or nonessential to our core purpose or mission....

In the midst of all the prognosticating that is taking place in church, I believe we are missing the one element key to the whole conversation: *the need for confession and a renewed desire to seek the heart of God.*

— Thomas J. Bickerton, *What Are We Fighting For?*

---

1. Inspired to Do Our Part

For God will command his angels concerning you to guard you in all your ways.

(Psalm 91:11)

In our family, there is a prized possession that sits on a shelf in my parents' home. It is a plain green teapot.

This simple ceramic antique once belonged to my grandparents. Back in the days when work was scarce and it was difficult to make ends meet, they would store extra money in the old green teapot. It was their tithe money. Believing completely in the biblical model of stewardship, my grandparents would faithfully place their tithe in the green teapot after each payday.

Each Sunday they would place money from the teapot in the offering plate at church. But on other occasions, opportunities for ministry would knock at the door of their home. A neighbor would drop by and, in the course of the conversation, would confess that she didn't have any money for groceries. Before the conversation ended, there was money placed in her hands for some potatoes and a gallon of milk. It came from the teapot.

My grandfather was a Korean War veteran. While stationed in Korea as a part of the Occupational Forces, he fell in love with the people there. Wanting to return as a missionary but never finding the way to make it happen, my grandfather instead sponsored a Korean orphan each year. The money came from the teapot.

One year a family friend was abandoned by her husband. She was left alone to care for their five children. My grandparents helped her go to nursing school so she could provide for her family. Their support came from the teapot.

For years no one in our family knew about the teapot. My grandparents humbly went about living out their faith without the need for recognition. They were simply being faithful. In recent years, however, the story of the teapot has been shared as a way of carrying on our rich family heritage.

In speaking about his parents my father says, "No matter what my parents had, they believed that God would take care of them. The teapot became a great lesson for me. God will take care of you if you only believe." That old green antique serves as a vivid reminder for our family about setting priorities and trusting in God's care.

As you seek to do your part in your church and community, remember that God will take care of you even when you wonder how you will make it through. Pause today and say a word of thanks for the gift of grace and God's abiding care.

Thank you, God, for providing for me in ways that I cannot even understand or comprehend. Amen.

---

2. Integrating God into Our Actions

Now, during those days he went out to the mountain to pray; and he spent the night in prayer to God.

(Luke 6:12)

I long to find right answers in the midst of difficult issues. Desperate to find just the right thing to say, I often find myself resorting to knee-jerk reactions rather than well-thought-out responses. I am tempted to fire off an immediate answer when I should have taken the time to ponder and pray. Sometimes immediacy is not wisdom and a quick response is not good leadership.

In his book *The View from a Hearse,* Joseph Bayly shares an experience of comfort he received when one of his children died suddenly:

> I was sitting, torn by grief. Someone came and talked
> to me of God's dealings, of why it happened, of hope
> beyond the grave. He talked constantly; he said things
> I knew were true. I was unmoved, except to wish he'd
> go away. He finally did. Another came and sat beside
> me. He didn't talk. He didn't ask leading questions. He
> just sat beside me for an hour and more, listening when
> I said something, answered briefly, prayed simply, left.
> I was moved. I was comforted. I hated to see him go.[1]

We long for easy answers to difficult questions and situations. While quick fixes are often desired, they can cause more harm than good. Taking the long view of things means taking extra care to pray when there are no quick answers and listen when silence feels awkward.

There is a simple first step: allow yourself to be in the moment and invite the presence of God to direct your words and actions. The simple prayer "God direct my path in this situation" can create just enough pause to allow God to do what God does best.

The perfect answer to a big problem may not be found quickly. Today, start with a few simple, intentional steps. Stop and speak a sentence prayer at the top of every hour. Memorize a verse of Scripture each day. Speak a word of encouragement to a coworker or a kind word to a stranger. Get into the habit of letting God use you to be a blessing to someone else.

When you do, you might just find that the big answers will start to be revealed in surprising and exciting ways.

What have you got to lose?

God, bless me with your presence today. Direct my path so that I may be a blessing to others. Amen.

---

3. Isolation or Integration?

So we, who are many, are one body in Christ, and individually we are members one of another.

(Romans 12:5)

Building and maintaining community is a challenge in today's world. For as much connectivity as there is in our culture, there is so much that isolates us from one another. To find a way to be together and stay together is at the heart of what it means to be the body of Christ.

Dr. Eugene Brice tells the story about a minister who returned to visit a church he had once served. He ran into Bill, who had been an elder and leader in the church, but who wasn't around anymore.

The pastor asked, "Bill, what happened? You used to be there every time the doors opened."

"Well, Pastor," said Bill, "a difference of opinion arose in the church. Some of us couldn't accept the final decision and we established a church of our own."

"Is that where you worship now?" asked the pastor.

"No," answered Bill, "we found that there, too, the people were not faithful, and a small group of us began meeting in a rented hall at night."

"Has that proven satisfactory?" asked the minister.

"No, I can't say that it has," Bill responded. "Satan was active even in that fellowship, so my wife and I withdrew and began to worship on Sunday at home by ourselves."

"Then at last you have found inner peace?" asked the pastor.

"No, I'm afraid we haven't," said Bill. "Even my wife began to develop ideas I was not comfortable with, so now she worships in the northeast corner of the living room, and I am in the southwest."[2]

This humorous story has a definite thread of truth in it. If you want to find fault with someone or something, you will most likely succeed. There are no perfect people, churches, or organizations to be found. But if you want to find community in the midst of good people who sometimes make mistakes, you will be blessed to discover that the Holy Spirit is at work shaping and molding communities of faith into the likeness of Jesus. If you look for perfection, you will be searching forever. If you look for a community of faith filled with people just like you who are searching for meaning and what matters most in their lives, you won't have to look very far.

What are you looking for?

O God, help me not fall victim to those things that isolate me from others. Guide me as I seek a deeper sense of community with others. Amen.

4. Depending on One Another

"I truly understand that God shows no partiality, but in every nation anyone who fears him and does what is right is acceptable to him."

(Acts 10:34)

One of my best friends is a person with whom I share very little in common. He was raised in the city. I was raised in a small town. He has a passion for soccer. I have a passion for baseball. He works in a secular field. I work in the church. The list goes on and on.

We can argue with one another over the smallest subjects. Yet there is a deep-seated respect between us. As they say, we have each other's back. We know that we can depend on one another in spite of the differences between us. If someone comes after my friend, first they will have to come through me.

In East Africa, there are two animals that share very little in common. The mighty rhinoceros is feared by most creatures in the wild except for one, the buffalo bird. Watching rhinos in their natural environment, you often see birds perched on their backs. From time to time these birds begin pecking at the back of the rhino similar to the way a woodpecker works away at an old tree. Others fly around the head of the rhino. If I were a rhino, I would be terribly annoyed! Yet the rhino does not attack the buffalo bird. The two of them have an understanding.

From birth, a rhinoceros has very poor eyesight. In addition, the rhino's body is covered with uncontrollable parasites. The buffalo bird loves parasites and does the rhino a great favor by eating them. Likewise, when there is danger in the area, the buffalo bird lets out a shrill call, warning the rhino. In return for this service, the buffalo birds are protected from their natural enemies by one of Africa's largest mammals. This arrangement is mutuality at its best—two very different creatures looking out for each other.

I have found that, at times, very different people come into our lives to broaden our horizons and reveal the magnitude of God's creation. We can easily reject them because they are so different from us. Or, we can see them as a gift from God. Eventually we might even discover that they have our backs.

Pray today that God might reveal to you someone who will broaden your perspective and complement your life, even if you don't agree with them.

God, move me today from independence to dependence. Help me to see the value in those with whom I do not always agree. Amen.

---

5. Sharing the Gift Within Us

For I am longing to see you so that I may share with you some spiritual gift to strengthen you.

(Romans 1:11)

I believe that there is a longing in every soul for purpose and meaning. That longing, when realized, can open an individual to a world previously unknown and unseen. We who embrace the Christian faith have been given a precious gift. None of us acquired it on our own. It was, in one form or another, given to us as a gift. The invitation to receive that gift changed our lives. The invitation we offer to others can and does have the same effect.

The story is told of a wise woman who was traveling in the mountains and found a precious stone in a stream. The next day she met another traveler who was hungry, and the wise woman opened her bag to share her food. The hungry traveler saw the precious stone and asked the woman to give it to him. She did so without hesitation. The traveler left, rejoicing in his good fortune. He knew the stone was worth enough to give him security for a lifetime. But a few days later he came back to return the stone to the wise woman. "I've been thinking," he said. "I know how valuable the stone is, but I give it back in the hope that you can give me something even more precious. Give me what you have within you that enabled you to give me the stone."[3]

The presence of Christ within us is that which enables us to do, at times, the extraordinary. It takes us where we are and lifts us to a place where we can, with confidence, see possibilities that we could not see before. The real gift is not what we have in our possession. The real gift is the ability to give ourselves away to others. That gift is only possible when we invite the presence of Christ to dwell deep within us.

Today, invite Jesus to come and bless your life again. Today, consider how you might invite someone else into the heart of God's love.

O God, give me what you have that will enable me to give what I have to others. Amen.

Week Two

THREE REMINDERS FOR THE JOURNEY

Who will separate us from the love of Christ? Will hardship, or distress, or persecution, or famine, or nakedness, or peril, or sword?... No, in all these things we are more than conquerors through him who loved us. For I am convinced that neither death, nor life, nor angels, nor rulers, nor things present, nor things to come, nor powers, nor height, nor depth, nor anything else in all creation, will be able to separate us from the love of God in Christ Jesus our Lord.

(Romans 8:35, 37-39)

We are so eager to arrive at the answers that we often fail to remind ourselves of the simple yet significant principles required to create an atmosphere of genuine spiritual discernment.… The end result or destination is attainable only if we have prepared for the journey that will get us there.…

In the midst of these uneasy and uncertain times of discernment, it is important to remember that we have not yet arrived and that there are many more discoveries to be made along the way. You and I are a work in progress, created by God and shaped by others whom God prepares, equips, and sends to bless us each step of the way. They are the ones who remind us that God is not through with us yet. They are the ones who reassure us that we are loved and that they will never let us go.

—Thomas J. Bickerton, *What Are We Fighting For?*

1. Lighten Up, Loosen Up, and Have a Little Fun

If you think that you are wise in this age, you should become fools so that you may become wise.
(1 Corinthians 3:18)

A few years ago two of my children joined me in a month-long driving adventure. I carefully mapped out our route and selected all of the spectacular sights that we were going to experience. Many represented some of the most famous places in the United

States. I was sure they would provide for us a long-lasting series of "memory makers."

On one particular day we found our planned destination, parked the car, and began walking. On the way we came across a street fair. At one display there were a series of plywood panels painted with goofy looking characters: cowboys, animals, and body builders. In each of the scenes, the heads of the characters were cut out, providing a spot for someone to insert their head and assume the posture of the character on the panel. We stopped at each one and took turns inserting our heads. We laughed and took pictures of one another assuming these various positions. It was a good day in the midst of a great trip.

To this day, when we reflect upon this well-planned trip, one of the first things my kids say is, "Do you remember that day when we stopped in Kansas and took pictures in those goofy panels?" They encourage me to pull out the photographs and we laugh all over again. They thought the national parks were beautiful. But their best memory was what we did on an impulsive day of spontaneity when we veered from the schedule and got silly together!

We work very hard to plan out our lives and our schedules. We give ourselves just enough time to get between point A and point B. We determine what we think will bring us the best inspiration and blessing. Yet some of the most meaningful experiences we have are the ones we cannot plan or predetermine. They happen when we loosen up just enough to experience them.

What is something you have wanted to do but haven't found a way to do it? How open are you to having your well-laid-out plans changed in a moment of inspiration or spontaneity? God has given us a great world, even in our own backyards, where we can lighten up, loosen up, and have a little fun. Grab hold of those spontaneous moments in life when you put everything on pause and let yourself experience something new, fresh, and unexpected.

Go ahead. I know you can do it!

God, free me from my preoccupations and lighten me up so that I may experience the fullness of your glory. Amen.

---

2. Intertwined with One Another

May the God of steadfastness and encouragement grant you to live in harmony with one another, in accordance with Christ Jesus, so that together you may with one voice glorify the God and Father of our Lord Jesus Christ.
(Romans 15:5-6)

Lewis Timberlake tells the story of a trip he once took to see California's giant sequoia trees. The guide pointed out the General Sherman—one of the tallest, widest, and longest-lived trees on the planet. This awe-inspiring tree began a conversation between Timberlake and the guide:

"I bet the roots on that tree are one hundred feet deep," I remarked to the guide.

"No, sir," he responded. "As a matter of fact, the sequoia tree has roots just barely under the ground."

"That's impossible," I exclaimed. "I'm a country boy, and I know better than that. If the roots don't grow deep into the earth, strong winds will blow the trees over."

"Not sequoia trees, Mr. Timberlake. They only grow in groves, and their roots intertwine with each other under the surface of the earth. So, when the strong winds come they hold each other up."[4]

There are some people in the church that could be described as possessing shallow roots. But in today's ever-changing and often tumultuous world, even those who possess strong roots are challenged to maintain their faith when the strong winds begin to blow.

How good it is to know that whether our roots are shallow or deep, we have one another to lean on in the midst of great uncertainty. The church at its best is a community of believers who intertwine their lives with one another and discover strength and courage that could not be possessed alone.

What is the state of your spiritual roots? Do they run deep or are they shallow and in need of the assurance that interdependency on others can provide?

What is the state of your church's spiritual roots? When the strong winds of life begin to blow, does your church serve as reinforcement in the midst of the storm? How well do you hold one another up? The church is at its best when it works together, with faith and intentionality, to intertwine the roots of its people, and fashions itself through support and collaboration into the body of Christ.

May it be so.

Loving God, connect my roots with the faith of others so that our lives might be strengthened together. Amen.

---

3. Working Together

> *"The glory that you have given me I have given them, so that they may be one, as we are one."*
>
> (John 17:22)

Marty Kaare tells a wonderful story about the beauty and innocence of working together:

> During a Vacation Bible School, a new student was brought into a teacher's preschool class. The boy had only one arm and the teacher had no time to prepare his class from making inappropriate remarks to the little boy.
>
> The teacher had the kids do their usual closing. Interlocking their fingers they said: "This is the church, and this is the steeple. Open the doors…" The teacher, to her horror, realized she had done the very thing she feared her kids would do.
>
> As she stood there, embarrassed, a little girl sitting next to the boy put her left hand up to the boy's right hand and said, "Davey, let's make the church together."[5]

What a wonderful visual: two children putting their hands together and creating the symbol of the church. Can you see it? From the roof to the steeple to the wiggling fingers of the people, two separate hands making the replica of one little church.

The church we love cannot survive unless we adopt the same attitude. "Hey, what do you say we come together and make us a church?" This is our opportunity and our choice. We can either fight one another or find a way to come together. We can stir the pots of controversy and gossip or stir the fires of unity and support. We can highlight one another's mistakes and shortcomings or bear witness to one another's blessings and gifts.

With the right attitude, blessed by the Spirit of our God, we can join our hands together to build the roof, erect the steeple, and assemble the people.

"Hey, Christian, let's make the church together."

God, bring us together as one people under the umbrella of your grace and love. Amen.

---

4. Finding a Way to Believe

Jesus looked at them and said, "For mortals it is impossible, but not for God; for God all things are possible."
(Mark 10:27)

One of the most important reminders on the journey to discovering what matters most is that God can use all of us in ways we cannot even begin to imagine. Miracles happen that we cannot explain. Unlikely people rise up to do extraordinary things when we least expect it. It is so important to remember that with God, nothing is impossible.

In Lewis Carroll's *Through the Looking Glass*, there is a wonderful interchange between Alice and the Red Queen. Alice says, "There's no use trying, one *can't* believe impossible things." The Queen responds, "I daresay you haven't had much practice. When I was your age, I always did it for half-an-hour a day. Why, sometimes I've believed as many as six impossible things before breakfast."[6]

We all have points in the journey when we struggle with faith. When we do, we are like most of the people described in the Bible. Whether it was someone who struggled with how to get across the Red Sea, convert the residents of Ninevah, or spread the word to the Gentiles, people have always struggled to trust God. When someone says, "We can't," seeds of doubt are planted. When someone says, "Yes we can," faith has been demonstrated.

I came across a story about a train that was moving fast in the midst of a raging thunderstorm. The tension among the passengers was evident. However, in the corner, there was a little boy sitting by himself completely unaware of the storm. One of the passengers asked the boy, "Excuse me son, aren't you afraid to travel on such a stormy night?" The little boy smiled at the passenger and said, "No ma'am, I'm not afraid. My daddy's the engineer."[7]

Remember today that God is in charge, and with that assurance we can find a way through the storm together. We may not know the future, but we do know who holds our hands. Thanks be to God!

God, help me to put aside my doubts and believe more fully in you. Amen.

---

5. We Are a Work in Progress

> *I am about to do a new thing;*
> *now it springs forth, do you not perceive it?*
>
> (Isaiah 43:19)

The story is told of a young boy who loved to tinker. He took apart everything he could get his hands on. One day the boy's grandmother found an old clock that no longer worked. She gave it to her grandson with the hope that he would somehow find a way to make it work again. The boy dove into the project with gusto. He took the clock apart, cleaned all the parts, and carefully put them back together again. Remarkably the clock once again worked like it was brand new.

Suppose, however, that this story unfolded differently. What if the boy had refused to accept the clock, claiming that it was not worth the effort to fix? Or, what if he took the clock, put it on a shelf, and never touched it again? If either of these options were inserted into the story, the boy would never have enjoyed the benefit of a working clock and the satisfaction of knowing that he had made it work once again.

Similarly, God has offered us the gift of the church. It once worked very well and was extremely effective in fulfilling its purpose. But today in certain places, the church just doesn't seem to work like it once did.

Today we are being offered the chance to take the church apart, clean its parts, oil its machinery, reset its timing, add a new piece of technology, and put it back together again. Those who are willing are the ones who believe that the church of Jesus Christ can run just as well as it did in years gone by.

If we refuse the gift, or simply accept it and place it on a shelf, the church will eventually wither away into a dust-gathering antique. But if we accept the gift and are determined with God's help to make it work, the end result can be a church of vitality, joy, and promise.

You and I are a work in progress. So is our church. Today, offer a prayer for your church. Pray that God might reveal to you the places that need some tinkering and refurbishing. In that prayer ask God to use you to be an instrument of restoration and transformation.

If we do the work of transformation, perhaps the old watch slogan can be used to describe our church: "It takes a licking but keeps on ticking."

O God, use me to be an instrument of transformation in the church that I love. Amen.

Week Three

DISCERNING WHAT MATTERS MOST

Therefore, since we are surrounded by so great a cloud of witnesses, let us also lay aside every weight and the sin that clings so closely, and let us run with perseverance the race that is set before us, looking to Jesus the pioneer and perfecter of our faith, who for the sake of the joy that was set before him endured the cross, disregarding its shame, and has taken his seat at the right hand of the throne of God.

(Hebrews 12:1-2)

When it comes to determining what matters most for us as the church in this generation, the great temptation we face is wanting to get to the end result without properly and carefully laying the foundation, paving the road, and navigating the terrain. It is easy to say, "I feel this is what matters most. This is what I'm fighting for!" It is far more difficult to earnestly search in community for what matters most and determine together how we are going to fight to maintain those principles. This search is called discernment....

I believe that God, as our creator, longs for us to develop the same discerning spirit—the ability not only to distinguish between right and wrong but also to determine those things that are worth fighting for in the midst of the complexities of our world. This process of spiritual discernment is a discipline.

–Thomas J. Bickerton, *What Are We Fighting For?*

---

1. Don't Wait

And all of us, with unveiled faces, seeing the glory of the Lord as though reflected in a mirror, are being transformed into the same image from one degree of glory to another; for this comes from the Lord, the Spirit.

(2 Corinthians 3:18)

The older I get, the more reluctant I am to change. I like my established rhythms and routines. They bring me a sense of comfort. Yet in this quickly changing world, waiting too long to make the adaptations necessary in order to stay relevant and vital can be disastrous.

The story is told about an eagle that was enjoying a beautiful but cold winter day flying across the mountains. After a while, the eagle grew tired and needed to rest. Spotting a log floating down a slow-moving river, the eagle felt that this was the perfect spot to enjoy a well-deserved rest. It was cold but the sun was shining, and the eagle thoroughly enjoyed the easy ride on the gentle stream. Before long, the quiet stream began to get choppy. Listening carefully, the eagle determined that there was a waterfall approaching. The eagle was one for adventure, so he decided to wait until the very last minute to fly off the log and back into the sky. He waited and waited until the log reached the edge of the waterfall. At the very last minute, the eagle spread his wings to fly, but it was too late! The bird's feet had frozen to the log.[8]

Adapting to changing circumstances requires the ability to free our feet from the frozen logs of our established norms. Often we try to hold on as long as we can to the things that make us comfortable only to find out that we have waited too long. Whether it's life transitions or new circumstances, job choices or family decisions, health matters or personal finance, faith stances or everyday practices, it's important to be able to adapt in order to thrive. How often have you resorted to the often-used statement, "That's just the way I am"?

Where are you frozen to a log? Are you so set in your ways that you are unable to relate to those around you? Start small today and work your way up to the needed changes that will make you more open and receptive to the ways God is currently at work all around you.

*Open my eyes and ears today, O God, to the ways in which you call
me to adapt and change. Amen.*

---

2. Look Back and Give Thanks

*"Let the little children come to me; do not stop them; for
it is to such as these that the kingdom of God belongs."*
(Mark 10:14)

Growing up in our family there was one thing you could
count on: we were going to church. Sunday morning, Sunday
night, and Wednesday night were standard expectations.

Most of the time I didn't mind it so much. The times I hated,
though, were the Sunday nights when our pastor was not present. That meant that the lay leader of the church would lead the
service. What I didn't like about it was that at some point in the
service, the lay leader would speak up and say, "Now we're going
to ask 'Little Tommy Bickerton' to pray." I was only eight or nine
years old, and yet he would ask me to pray!

I tried to become clever in my anticipation of his request.
I would pretend to be asleep. I would fake being sick. I would
hide under the pew. But rest assured, at some point he would say,
"We're going to ask 'Little Tommy Bickerton' to pray!" I hated
when that lay leader said that!

Much happened to me after those Sunday nights in church.
I grew and followed through with my calling from God to be a

pastor. Years later I returned to my home area as a district superintendent. Once the moving van left, I paid a visit to a patient in the local hospital. I walked into the room and saw a man who was dying. It was that same lay leader from my childhood.

During the next few minutes, I shared with him how terrified I was each time he called on me when I was a boy. But then I had a chance to say something to him that I had never said before: "I've come here today to thank you for teaching me how to pray." They were words that were long overdue. I didn't realize it when I was young, but as I grew I knew that the chance he took in asking me to pray paid off in the long run. He believed in me even when I didn't believe in myself.

Looking back, I give thanks for him and others who took a chance on me and helped me become the person I am today.

Who are the people who helped to form and shape your life? Look back, remember, and give thanks.

O God, thank you today for the persons who have helped to mold me into your likeness. Amen.

---

3. Seizing the Opportunity Before You

"For you will be his witness to all the world of what you have seen and heard."

(Acts 22:15)

A few years ago, several of our clergy friends and their families spent a week together on vacation. One night we decided to head out for an evening meal together. We were seated at a large round table. The conversation was lively, and everyone was feeling very relaxed. We placed our order and settled in for a good night together.

When our waitress delivered the meal, a curious conversation unfolded. The question at hand was centered on who was going to pray before we ate. Which pastor would rise to the occasion? Or would it be one of the children? Perhaps a spouse would step up to the plate and offer thanks for our meal. The conversation turned into a debate. "You pray," someone said to me. "No, you should pray," I said to another. "No, perhaps we should ask one of the kids," another chimed in.

To our surprise, an unfamiliar voice spoke up. It was our waitress. "I'll pray for you," she said. She reached out her hands to us and we listened as our waitress offered thanks to God for the very meal that she was about to serve us.

When the prayer ended, we couldn't help but ask about the courage it took to offer herself in this way. She explained that at her church they encourage the parishioners to be courageous and bold in offering a public witness of their faith. As she heard us debating who would pray, she thought to herself, *Why not me?* She seized the opportunity and provided a blessing that we will never forget.

Often we defer prayers and public witnessing to the "called ones" in our midst. Yet every one of us is "called" to a ministry that bears witness to the love of God in our hearts. Sometimes that witness is in bold and dramatic acts of faithfulness. Other times it is a result of a well-thought-out strategy. And sometimes it happens through a simple, spontaneous prayer that no one expects.

Ask God today to give you the courage to increase your public witness. Be looking for those times when you can seize an opportunity to bless someone with the grace and love of God. You might just be surprised at how God can and will use you.

Why not you? Why not today?

Lord, give me the courage and the opportunity to bless someone's life today. Use me to be an instrument of your will. Amen.

---

4. Searching on the Right Level

"Child, why have you treated us like this! Look,
your father and I have been searching for you in great
anxiety." Jesus said to them, "Why were you searching
for me? Did you not know that I must be in my Father's
house?"

(Luke 2:48-49)

Our family vacation was interrupted one year by my daughter's need to return home in order to begin her next semester in college. Elizabeth's trip home required a cross-country flight that meant getting to the airport extremely early in the morning.

Droopy eyed, my son T.J. and I took her to the airport, parked the car, and escorted her to the security checkpoint.

After our goodbyes, T.J. and I made our way back to the parking garage only to discover that our car was missing. We went to the exact spot where we had parked the car, and it was not there! Our sense of wonderment turned into a feeling of panic as we went from one spot in the garage to another.

Finally, totally exasperated, we got on the elevator to go down to the ground level and report our missing vehicle. On the way down, the elevator doors opened and a gentleman got in. Looking out through the open door, T.J. said, "Look there, Dad. Is that our car?"

It was. When we got to the car we discovered that we had searched the exact place where we had parked the car. The only trouble was we were on the wrong level. The car was right where we had parked it. But our early morning drowsiness and lack of attention had taken us to the wrong floor!

At times our search for meaning leads us to a place where we firmly believe that truth resides. Yet it just doesn't feel right. We think we've taken all of the right steps and gone in the right direction. But sometimes, in the process of discerning what matters most we discover that while we are in the general area, we've gotten off on the wrong floor.

There isn't just one level where truth and meaning reside. Sometimes the right answer is found at different points in the journey. We just have to be ready and willing to search for what matters most on the right level.

Are you hunting for truth and meaning in your life? Are you frustrated because you can't seem to find them? Try searching on a different level today. Think outside the box of your comfort zone. You might just discover that you are able to connect the dots in a way you never dreamed you could.

Ever present God, help me to trust you more each day as I search for truth and meaning in my life. Amen.

---

5. Keeping Watch for the Nonessentials

"Be on guard so that your hearts are not weighed down with dissipation and drunkenness and the worries of this life, and that day does not catch you unexpectedly."
(Luke 21:34)

Sometimes the very best work that we can do becomes diluted when we lose our sense of focus and purpose. Resting on our laurels or assuming that we are stronger than we really are can easily contribute to the loss of what matters most.

Henry Emerson Foscick often made reference to the Great Wall of China, one of the most fascinating wonders of the world. It was built 214 years before the birth of Christ in order to protect the vulnerable north border of China from the raids of Mongolian horsemen.

The wall, which is the longest structure made with human hands, still stands today, zigzagging its way through the hills of north China. It is estimated that as many as one million people died building the wall.

When the wall was finished, it appeared to be unconquerable. It was just too big and overpowering to be scaled. Yet history tells us that the enemy got past the Great Wall three times. How? Not by breaking it down or going around it. The enemy got past the wall by bribing the gatekeepers!

Commenting on this reality, Fosdick once said, "It was the human element that failed. What collapsed was character which proved insufficient to make the great structure men had fashioned really work."[9]

God has blessed us with a great church and a wonderful opportunity to work for God's kingdom in the name of Jesus Christ. Yet this work often fails, not because of God or structures or well-crafted plans. The work of God's kingdom often fails because of us. We run the risk of being bribed and seduced to compromise our faith.

But here's the good news! The work of God succeeds when God's people see the need and do what has to be done. The wall of faith remains intact when we put aside the things that separate us and focus on the things that bring us unity and strength. When we sift out the nonessentials, we reinforce and strengthen that which matters the most.

Today pray that you can be a strong gatekeeper who is not bribed by the temptations of the world.

Strengthen me, O Lord, so that I can keep my focus on the things that matter most. Amen.

Week Four

FILLING IN THE BLANK WITH THE ESSENTIALS

As you therefore have received Christ Jesus the Lord, continue to live your lives in him, rooted and built up in him and established in the faith, just as you were taught, abounding in thanksgiving.

See to it that no one takes you captive through philosophy and empty deceit, according to human tradition, according to the elemental spirits of the universe, and not according to Christ. For in him the whole fullness of deity dwells bodily, and you have come to fullness in him, who is the head of every ruler and authority.

(Colossians 2:6-10)

We've seen that the life of Jesus is our benchmark when discerning what matters most—the standard or measure that helps us link our actions with the will and plan of God. The idea is to connect the principles that Jesus lived and taught with the practical ways we "do church."...

If we are to reclaim our vitality and purpose as representatives of the message Jesus placed into our hands, we must discern and examine the essentials—those principles and passions we are to live out until Jesus returns. In his name, we are called to be the conveyors of things such as grace, relationships, joy, and hope. If we won't, who will?

–Thomas J. Bickerton, *What Are We Fighting For?*

---

1. A Simple Reminder

"Let anyone among you who is without sin be the first to throw a stone at her."

(John 8:7)

My office is a museum. Over the years I have collected many items that are on display. I have a vast collection of books, diplomas, trinkets, and memorabilia. The certificates from my baptism and church membership hang proudly next to ones from my ordination. There is a shelf that remembers each of the schools I attended and the church appointments I have served. There is even a John Wesley bust from the early 1800s sitting next to the latest bobble head of our denomination's founding father.

When people enter my office, they always ask many questions about what they see. Rarely do they ask about one of my most cherished symbols. Sitting on a shelf near the conference table where I often conduct difficult and challenging conversations is a rock. It is a large stone, grey in color with many jagged edges. It has no sentimental value and would be appraised to be worth nothing. It is just a rock.

If I chose to use the rock as a weapon, I could cause significant injury to someone. Instead, I use it as a daily reminder. My words can also cause injury. My actions can inflict pain. My judgments can unfairly condemn. The rock sits in prominent view as a daily reminder: "You who are without sin, cast the first stone."

My oldest son carries a small stone in his pocket. The stone dates back to a time when his grandfather was paying the bill at the end of a meal. While he was shuffling through the change in his pocket, T.J. noticed a smooth, shiny rock among the coins. "Paw Paw, why do you have that rock in your pocket?" he asked. In a very quiet and compassionate voice, a grandfather shared a simple word of teaching with his grandson: "You who are without sin, cast the first stone." The lesson had an enduring impact. Today, every time T.J. puts his hand into his pocket, he remembers.

So must we. Life is filled with daily temptations to retaliate with unkind words and actions. Before we know what has happened, a conversation turns into an encounter where judgments are leveled and hurt is inflicted.

Perhaps this week you could find a rock for your shelf or a pebble for your pocket and use it as a reminder of what grace is all about. What we have been given, we are called to share.

Holy God, lessen my judgments and increase my love for others today. Amen.

---

2. Building an Honest Relationship

"So when you are offering your gift at the altar, if you remember that your brother or sister has something against you, leave your gift there before the altar and go; first be reconciled to your brother or sister, and then come and offer your gift."

(Matthew 5:23-24)

Early on I knew that one of the rough edges in my ministry was time management. At times I found myself having trouble navigating all the things that were coming my way. I had great intentions and wanted to do a good job. The problem was it often made me late for my next appointment.

Rather than improve, I developed the skill of being able to convince myself that being late was justifiable. Surely those who were waiting for me would understand!

One day I was once again late for my regular covenant group gathering. I entered the room armed with all my reliable excuses. The surgery took longer than expected. I ran into someone who really needed to talk. Traffic was horrendous.

When I explained my tardiness, a member of my covenant group spoke up. "You know," he said, "I'm really tired of hearing all of your excuses. Do you not realize that when you are ten minutes late for this meeting, that makes me ten minutes late for my next appointment? You are just a really poor time manager!"

But my covenant brother did not stop there. "Next month there is a time management seminar being put on by a nationally renowned group. I have signed you up for it and I want you to go." And then he said it: "I want you to be the best that you can be. You will not realize your full potential until you get ahold of this particular problem in your life."

Have you ever felt beaten up but loved in the same moment? I did. My friend had the courage to confront me with a problem but loved me enough to provide a potential solution. He didn't just satisfy his own frustration. He showed me that at the heart of his concern was love. It was for the sake of our relationship that he found the courage to deal with a flaw in my character.

Jesus did that quite often with his disciples. In the midst of their intimate relationship Jesus molded them into his likeness. Jesus said a very affirming word to Peter, "On this rock I will build my church." But he also had the courage to chastise him with the words, "Get behind me, Satan!" (Matthew 16:18, 23). He helped Peter see a vision for his life that required both affirmation and accountability. That took courage. But it also required relationship.

Today there is someone who needs to be loved into a better habit or lifestyle. Pray that you might have the courage to be honest. But also pray that you might build the kind of relationships that make that honesty possible.

Loving God, give me the courage I need to build lasting relationships that are built on honesty and love. Amen.

3. Building an Enduring Relationship

Some friends play at friendship
but a true friend sticks closer than one's nearest kin.
(Proverbs 18:24)

During my freshman year in college I found myself in a situation where my roommate and I were not seeing eye to eye. He was, and remains to this day, my friend. But we quickly discovered that although we were friends, we just couldn't live together.

That incompatibility often led me into the hallway of the dormitory where I would sit on the floor and study late at night. One night I left my room to assume my normal position on the floor and discovered someone else sitting nearby. Like me, he was having a hard time finding compatibility with his roommate.

A conversation ensued that was fun and engaging. It happened the next night as well and continued for many nights throughout the semester. At the end of our freshman year, my hallway friend and I decided that we would stop sitting on the floor and become roommates. We did, and a relationship began that has lasted to this day.

Today my college roommate and I live two different lives in two different cities. There are periods of time when we don't talk with regularity. But when we realize that we haven't talked in a while, we call. And when we do, a funny thing happens. We pick up right where we left off and talk as if we lived a few doors down the hallway rather than a few hundred miles away. In those moments, we once again sit on the floor and build a relationship that I believe will last a lifetime.

There are times on the journey when we don't feel comfortable with our surroundings. Pressures mount and controversies arise that cause us to feel alone and left out. Yet just down the hall there is someone facing similar pressures and heartaches. Just down the hall is someone who can understand and care. Just down the hall is a relationship that can endure for a lifetime.

Who is that person you haven't called in a while? Is there a person in your neighborhood who appears to be alone and unengaged? Perhaps it's a colleague at work who simply needs someone like you to sit on the floor with them and understand.

Grace is freely extended when we least expect it. We transmit grace the very same way. Sometimes it results in a relationship that lasts a lifetime.

Thank you, God, for relationships that endure the test of time. Help me to be a good friend. Amen.

---

4. Bearers of Hope

Rejoice in hope, be patient in suffering, persevere in prayer.

(Romans 12:12)

One of the all-time greats in the game of baseball was Babe Ruth. His 714 home runs and magnetic personality made "The Babe" the first true sports idol.

Ruth was revered as a New York Yankee. Yet as he grew older, his popularity began to wane as his skills diminished. Finally, the Yankees traded him to the Boston Braves. In one of his last games, Babe Ruth struck out each time he came up to bat. After allowing the opposing team to score several runs off of one of his errors, there arose an enormous storm of boos and catcalls from the crowd.

Just then one of the Babe's enduring fans, a small boy, jumped over the railing and ran toward his hero. With tears flowing from his cheeks, the boy threw his arms around Ruth's legs. The mighty Babe scooped up the little boy and hugged him. Taking his hand, Babe Ruth walked off the field with his lone supporter and greatest fan.[10]

Have you ever felt like you are being booed off the field as if nothing you say or do is right and no one seems to care? For whatever reason you feel alone and dejected, scorned and pushed aside. Life has dealt you a cruel blow and you wonder how you're going to make it through. Have you ever felt that way?

On days when I have felt a deep sense of loneliness and despair, it seems that God has always provided a way for me to once again find hope and encouragement. Often it has come from someone who loved and accepted me for who I was in that moment, not what I had done in previous times up to bat. When I could not find my way, God always sent someone to encourage and support me in my time of need.

When was the last time you jumped over the rail and embraced someone who was being booed off the field? Who needs you the most today? How can you be an angel of God who brings mercy and grace?

Today, open your eyes and ears to the people around you who need a word of hope and encouragement on the journey. You might just become the face of Christ to them in a moment of great need.

O God, use me today to be a blessing of hope and encouragement for someone in need. Amen.

---

5. Embracing Simple Joys

You have turned my mourning into dancing;
*   you have taken off my sackcloth*
*   and clothed me with joy,*
so that my soul may praise you and not be silent.
*   O LORD my God, I will give thanks to you forever*
                                    (Psalm 30:11-12)

I have always said that I wanted to be the kind of parent who enjoyed his children no matter their age. While it's true that your children sometimes disappoint you, I make no excuses: I am a doting parent! My children bring me great joy.

Our daughter has just been hired as an assistant principal. She has worked hard over the years to get the education and experience necessary to move into school administration. While it seems that she has been in school forever, it has begun to pay off. I'm very proud of Elizabeth.

Our third son is continuing his education in college. Admittedly, it is a rocky road for those who head off to school, and our son is no exception. He's had his struggles. But lately he has discovered that the light bulb needs a socket in order for the bulb to be illuminated. In other words, the light has come on for him and, all of a sudden, life has new meaning and purpose for him. I'm very proud of Ian.

In fact, I'm proud of all of our children. But with these two, a special thing has begun to take place. My daughter has started to become my colleague. She will call and say, "Hey Dad, I have a public speech coming up. Can I rehearse it with you?" My son has started to use me as his editor. He will call and say, "Hey Dad, I have a paper due. Could you read it for me?" In both cases, what I've discovered is that my children are adults with brilliant minds and unfolding careers. Parenting these days is not so much about instructing them as it is about simply sharing the joy of the journey with them.

I've always wanted to be the kind of parent who enjoyed his children no matter their age. Today, at this age, my kids bring me great joy.

Who is it that brings you great joy today? What is it that causes you to smile and find happiness? It could be a child, a colleague, a friend. It might be a blessing you received or one that you shared. Take the time today to let them know how much they have blessed your life.

Thank you, God, for the people and the blessings of life that bring me such great joy. Amen.

Week Five

PADDLING IN THE SAME CANOE

*For just as the body is one and has many members, and
all the members of the body, though many, are one body,
so it is with Christ. For in the one Spirit we were all
baptized into one body—Jews or Greeks, slaves or free—
and we were all made to drink of one Spirit.*

(1 Corinthians 12:12-13)

Paddling in the same boat requires a singular resolve that drives everyone to use their individual gifts while at the same time honoring the input and giftedness of the others who are paddling toward the same goal....

Every successful organization must find a platform or foundation upon which it can agree. Without a foundation, no building can be constructed. Without a baseline of commonality, an organization will fall into chaos and quickly crumble....Our foundation must be made up of the things that matter most—the essentials that give focus and clarity to our mission and ministry.
–Thomas J. Bickerton, *What Are We Fighting For?*

1. Unity in Diversity

"I therefore, the prisoner in the Lord, beg you to lead a life worthy of the calling to which you have been called, with all humility and gentleness, with patience, bearing with one another in love."

(Ephesians 4:1-2)

There is an old Hindu fable about six blind men who had never before seen an elephant. One day the villagers told them that there was an elephant in the village.

They had no idea what an elephant was, so they decided to go and touch it.

Touching the elephant's leg, the first man said, "Hey, the elephant is a pillar."

Touching the tail, the second man said, "Oh, no! It is a rope."

"I disagree," said the third man said as he touched the trunk of the elephant. "It is the thick branch of a tree."

"Absolutely not," said the fourth blind man as he touched the ear of the elephant. "It is like big hand fan," he exclaimed.

"It is a huge wall," said the fifth man who touched the belly of the elephant.

"No, sir," said the sixth man who was touching the elephant's tusk. "It is a solid pipe."

The six men began to argue about the elephant. They each insisted that they were right. Suddenly a wise man was passing by. He stopped and asked them, "What is the matter?"

They said, "We cannot agree to what the elephant is like."

The wise man calmly explained to them, "All of you are right. The reason every one of you is telling it differently is because each one of you touched a different part of the elephant. The elephant actually has all those features you have described."

From that point on there was no more fighting because each person was able to sense that his singular viewpoint was one part of the full description of what an elephant really was.

There are times when we can see the truth very clearly. There are other times when we can't because of the different perspectives of those around us. Sometimes we agree. Sometimes we don't.

Rather than arguing like the blind men, perhaps we can find a way to honor one another's reasons and realize that their perspectives are part of the full picture we long to see. Today, pray that you can live in harmony with those who think differently than you.

Patient God, teach me to live in harmony with others who think differently than me. Amen.

2. Focusing on What Matters Most

*"But I say to you, Love your enemies and pray for those
who persecute you, so that you may be children of your
Father in heaven."*

(Matthew 5:44-45)

When I was growing up, my grandfather Bickerton was the
spiritual pillar of our family. Each Sunday he would sit with my
grandmother on the seventh pew on the right in our local church.
It didn't matter what the weather conditions were or who was in
the pulpit. They were always in church.

One Sunday morning I was walking out of church with my
grandfather when we came to the pastor's receiving line. When
our turn came, the pastor shook our hands. It was then that my
grandfather spoke. "I didn't agree with your sermon today," he
said. "It's not where I am or what I believe. But you need to know,
whether or not we agree, I pray for you every day."

As a boy, I was horrified by my grandfather's words! He
confronted the pastor right there in church! Yet the more I
thought about what he said, I began to sense the truth in my
grandfather's words.

You see, as long as my grandparents were alive, on their
kitchen table was a well-worn Bible with folded down edges
marking certain passages. Next to it was the latest devotional
book and the latest work from a famous evangelist. And sitting

somewhere in the middle of it all was a piece of paper—their prayer list. You could count on my name being on that list. So was my sister's name. So were my parents. And somewhere on that list you would also find the name of our pastor. You see, what my grandfather said to the pastor that Sunday morning was a fact. It didn't matter whether or not he agreed with what the pastor said or did. What mattered most was my grandfather's conviction that he should pray for his pastor each day. That's exactly what he did.

In the discernment of what matters most, it is critical that we find a way to sift out the nonessentials. Agreeing with one another is nice, but it is not necessary. What is necessary is finding a way to love one another when we disagree. It may even cause us to bow our heads and pray.

Today, think of someone with whom you do not see eye to eye. Pray that you have the courage to be honest with them about your feelings. Pray that you may also have the courage to pray. That is what matters most.

O God, teach me how to pray more genuinely and intentionally each day. Amen.

---

3. Working Together

Indeed, the body [of Christ] does not consist of one member but of many.

(1 Corinthians 12:14)

Not long after our daughter got her driver's license, we knew that she would need her own car. I thought that the search for an automobile had to be limited to price and safety. Elizabeth added a third priority. It had to be one she liked!

I took Elizabeth to the car lot and watched her eyes light up when she saw just the right car. I liked the price and the safety features. She liked the style and the color. Everything was perfect until she looked inside. To her dismay, her dream car had a manual transmission.

"I can't drive a standard!" Elizabeth exclaimed. I assured her that we would learn together and that she would eventually love driving it. I bought the car and we began the process of learning how to drive it.

I showed her how to simultaneously take your foot off of the clutch while putting your other foot on the accelerator. I taught her how to shift at just the right time and to not lose sight of her surroundings. We practiced night after night with one result: she hated it.

Finally one night I said, "I've taught you all the basics and we have practiced enough. It's time for you to do this on your own." She resisted mightily and told me that she would never be able to do this. After much urging, I sent her off on her own. There were times when she stalled the car going up a hill and other times when the engine would grind when the clutch wasn't depressed properly. But she kept on trying, and I kept on urging.

I will never forget the day when Elizabeth said, "I just love my car!" All of the practice and patience had paid off. She had not only mastered a new skill but also found a way to appreciate it. To this day she says that it was a hard lesson to learn but she is so grateful that she learned it. It proved to her that with determination she could do things she never dreamed possible.

There are lots of moving parts that have to be synchronized in order to work together as the body of Christ. In order to move forward, the right hand has to know what the left hand is doing. When it does, great things begin to happen. New horizons are seen and unknown possibilities are realized.

Today, pray about how you might "shift into another gear" by working together with others to build the body of Christ. With determination you might just be able to do things that you never dreamed were possible.

Bless me, Lord, with the ability to work together with others to build your Church. Amen.

---

4. Missing the Mark

So whether we are at home or away, we make it our aim to please [God].

(2 Corinthians 5:9)

Have you ever had a hard time hitting the mark? Good intentions combined with little thought and preparation can have disastrous consequences.

My dad tells the story of an annual family tradition when he was growing up. Each year the family would gather for

Thanksgiving at the rural country farm where his grandparents lived.

As a part of the tradition they would butcher a hog. Outside the farmhouse a large fire was built to roast the prize pig. As a young boy, each year my dad would watch them shoot the hog in preparation for the roast. This particular year though, my dad felt that he had reached the age where he could fire the shot. Persuading his father that his time had come, my dad eagerly took the .22 rifle in his hands. His grandfather showed him how to use the gun and where to aim. Then, after feeding the hog some corn, it was time to pull the trigger.

There was only one problem. Dad fired too low and failed to kill the pig. The hog squealed loudly and began to run. His grandfather had to chase down the pig and eventually put it out of its misery. Needless to say, it was some time before my dad was given the responsibility of shooting the Thanksgiving pig.

There are times when we feel that we know the right answer. There are other times when we have strong convictions about a matter and believe that our way is the preferable path. Yet our human inabilities often rise to the surface and reveal that our aim is not quite as good as we had thought. Perhaps we underestimated how our words might hurt someone. Maybe we didn't plan well, and our actions resulted in some unexpected consequences. With good intentions, we pulled the trigger, missed the target, and caused more harm than good.

Have you ever majored on a minor or minored on a major? Overestimating the importance of something can easily lead you or your group down the wrong path. Underestimating the value of something can quickly lead to damaged emotions and a breakdown of trust.

Take careful aim today. Is the right target clearly in sight? Is it worth the effort? Have you listened and learned well from those around you? Before you pull the trigger today, pause just long enough to make sure you've considered all the options and the potential consequences.

Lord, give me clear vision and focus today as I represent you. Help me to aim at the right target. Amen.

---

5. Let Nothing Stand in the Way

I press on toward the goal for the prize of the heavenly call of God in Christ Jesus.

(Philippians 3:14)

When we undertake the challenge of determining what matters most, it is important for us to have the courage to let nothing stand in the way of realizing it.

There is an interesting reality about my father. One of his favorite pastimes is fishing on a lake, and one of his favorite vacation spots is the beach. My dad absolutely loves the water, but curiously, he cannot swim.

Each year my family would vacation at our favorite beach. Dad would wade into the water as deep as he could go and ride the waves. Mom would keep a watchful, nervous eye on him, always afraid that the undertow might catch him off guard and drag him under.

One year we were lying on the beach when a stir arose among the people. To our amazement a shark had surfaced just off shore. To our shock, the shark was between my sister, who was in the water, and the shore. Before any of us could react, my father ran to the water. He had one mission—to bring my sister back to shore safely. It did not matter whether or not he could swim. What mattered most was my sister.

This story has a happy ending. The shark disappeared and my sister was not harmed. For that we are grateful. Beyond that, however, was the inspiration found that day. I learned what it meant to put yourself at risk for someone you love. I learned about priorities and not letting anything get in the way of fulfilling them. I learned about rising above great handicaps and obstacles when you have focus and determination. And I learned that there are days when you had better sift out what is nonessential in order to preserve what is really important.

There are days when it seems that we are living in shark-infested waters. There is a lot standing in the way of us finding peace, hope, vitality, and joy. Now more than ever it is important for us to focus on what matters most and find a way to not let anything get in the way of achieving it.

Go ahead. Wade into the water. As you go, rest assured that God has promised that we will never be left alone and that nothing will separate us from God's love in Jesus Christ.

Grant to me, almighty God, the ability to determine what matters most and to not let anything stand in the way of achieving it. Amen.

Week Six

FINISHING WITH LOVE

Love never ends. But as for prophecies, they will come to an end; as for tongues, they will cease; as for knowledge, it will come to an end. For we know only in part, and we prophesy only in part; but when the complete comes, the partial will come to an end. When I was a child, I spoke like a child, I thought like a child, I reasoned like a child; when I became an adult, I put an end to childish ways. For now we see in a mirror, dimly, but then we will see face to face. Now I know only in part; then I will know fully, even as I have been fully known. And now faith, hope, and love abide, these three; and the greatest of these is love.

(1 Corinthians 13:8-13)

When I think about who we are, I am amazed at the enduring love of our creator God who has had every reason to abandon the covenant and end the relationship. But in spite of our handicaps and flaws, God continues to embrace us with a love that will not let us go. And in those moments when we find ourselves on life support like an infant in an incubator, wondering how we are going to take the next step in the journey, God reaches through the open door and touches us with amazing grace and an awesome love. It is in those moments—in the midst of the sterile and technically advanced environment of our world—that we, the children of God, feel the warmth of God's touch....

When we make love a part of "all things," it is a non-negotiable aspect of every conversation, debate, and discernment process. When we make love a part of "all things," it is the driver for our devotion and our behavior. Even when we fall short of this mandate due to our human limitations and sinful nature, we make love a part of "all things" by repenting and seeking forgiveness. Love is ultimately what matters most.

–Thomas J. Bickerton, *What Are We Fighting For?*

1. In All Things, Love

"[Love] bears all things, believes all things, hopes all things, endures all things. Love never ends."

(1 Corinthians 13:7-8)

Funny things happen to people when they leave home for the first time. Some come to a deeper appreciation for the things they have left behind. Some walk away and begin to forge a new path for their future. And some experiment with what it means to be on their own and face the consequences of unwise decisions.

While I was not a rebel, I did encounter a few bumps on the road when I left home. During my first year of college, I found myself having a very animated conversation on the phone with my mother over one of my ill-advised decisions. The possibility for resolution didn't seem very likely as our interchange grew more heated. In a moment of frustration, we both said goodbye rather abruptly and finished the call. No sooner had I hung up when my phone suddenly rang. When I answered, my mom simply said, "I forgot to tell you that I love you."

In that moment I came to a new realization. My mother always ended every conversation with those words. It didn't matter whether she agreed with a decision I had made. No matter the day or time, my mom has always ended every conversation with three simple words, "I love you."

What would it look like if we took the same approach each day? It may not be that we end every conversation with the words "I love you," but perhaps we could enter into every day with love as the motivator for every conversation and meeting. It doesn't mean that we like everything that people do. But it does mean that we are so aware of God's love for us that we find ourselves falling in love with the world and the people God has created. My mother hasn't always liked the decisions I have made, but I am keenly aware that in all things, my mother loves me. She's made it a point to remind me every day, no matter the circumstances.

The Apostle Paul wrote, "[Love] bears all things, believes all things, hopes all things, endures all things. Love never ends" (1 Corinthians 13:7-8). This was written as a response to the awareness of God's great, enduring, and consistent love.

I wonder what you might write as a response to the awareness of God's claim on your life and God's call to make disciples of others.

It might be as simple as *I love you.*

Loving God, help me to see beyond the circumstances so that I may love you and others in all things. Amen.

---

2. A Voice in the Darkness

"Let love be genuine; hate what is evil, hold fast to what is good; love one another with mutual affection."
(Romans 12:9-10)

I was one of those fortunate young people who didn't have an established curfew. My parents believed that if I didn't abuse the privilege, they could extend a measure of trust to me.

Every so often, I would come home to find that all the lights had been turned off and my parents had gone to bed. Respecting their need for sleep, I would quietly tiptoe into the bathroom to brush my teeth, making sure that I made no sounds that would disturb them. Finally, I would undress, gently ease into my bed, and turn off my bedside lamp.

It was then, in the stillness and darkness of the night, that a curious and consistent thing would take place. From the bedroom down the hall my mom would quietly say, "Good night, Tom."

While my parents demonstrated their trust by going to bed while I was still out, they never stopped expressing concern and love for me in tangible ways. Though they trusted my ability not to abuse the privileges extended, they never could actually rest until they knew that I was safe at home.

There are times on the journey of life where the light is turned out and you begin to feel an utter sense of loneliness. The perils of life in this age make that possibility more of a reality each day. While there are many ways we are connected in this modern world, there is still a significant disconnect that leaves us wondering who will be our advocates and friends.

When those times happen, rest in the assurance that there is One who not only knows your name but watches over you with a love that will not let you go. When you least expect it, there is a voice that speaks a word of grace and reassurance.

Often when you ask the simple question "How are you?" the standard reply is, "Fine, thanks." But deep within the souls of those around us there lurks an insecurity, a sense of guilt, or an abiding fear that has disrupted that person's sense of peace and assurance. A gentle word in the midst of the darkness can go far to get someone over the hump and on the way to a recovery of self.

How might you be the voice of love to someone around you today? It may be as simple as saying, "Remember, you are loved."

Loving God, as you never forget to love me, help me to never forget to love others. Amen.

---

3. Above All Things, Love

[Nothing] will be able to separate us from the love of God in Christ Jesus our Lord.

(Romans 8:39)

One evening when I was growing up, I asked my parents for the keys to our only car. When permission was granted, I headed off for a fun evening of exploring what was happening in town.

On the way to pick up a friend, I came to a four-way stop sign. I turned on my left blinker and began to make the turn. Just then, a tape player I had brought with me slid off the passenger seat and fell on the floor. In a momentary reaction I reached down to pick it up but failed to acknowledge what was happening with my moving vehicle. I inadvertently made a U-turn and struck a parked car heading the other direction!

After calling my dad to explain the situation, he arrived on foot a few minutes later to survey the situation. After the dust settled, I tossed the car keys to my father, proclaiming that I didn't want to drive anymore.

The next night at supper, I was understandably quiet. My father initiated the conversation by saying, "What are your plans after supper?" When I indicated to him that I had none, he said to me, "Make some." In that moment, my dad did a remarkable thing. He slid the car keys next to my plate. "I don't care what you do," he said, "but after supper I want you to take the car out for a drive. You need to build back your confidence."

To this day I stand amazed at the courage it took for him to say those words. He believed in me even though I had made a mistake. He trusted me to not make the same mistake again. He restored my confidence.

In the years since that day I have often been confronted with similar moments when I have wondered if I have the courage to do as he did. It requires a great deal of strength to say, "I believe in you" rather than "How could you?"

We believe that God has embraced us with a love that will not let us go. We have the assurance that "[nothing in all creation] will be able to separate us from the love of God in Christ Jesus our Lord" (Romans 8:39).

We have been given the keys to the car even though we have a history of wrecking it.

Today, look for someone whose confidence has waned, someone who has fallen on hard luck, or someone who needs a reminder that they too are loved. Slide them a key that will once again unlock their trust and confidence.

You are loved with a love that will not let you go. Use that love in the way you love another today.

God, give me the courage to offer the key of love to someone who needs it today. Amen.

4. Sharing the Love

*Little children, let us love, not in word or speech, but in
truth and action.*

(1 John 3:18)

In my last local church, I had a purple bag that was used for
the weekly children's sermon. I would give the bag to a different
child each week and ask them to bring something that could be
used for my conversation with the children on Sunday. I never
knew what was in the bag before I opened it.

One Sunday, a group got together and placed something in
the purple bag as part of "Pastor Appreciation Sunday." The little
girl that had the bag handed it to me with a big smile on her face.
The bag was completely filled with Hershey Kisses. On top of the
kisses there was a note that said, "We wanted to give you some
kisses to remind you that you are loved."

A few weeks later, the same little girl asked me to come to
her kindergarten class and share what I did for a living. When I
inquired about what others had done, she told me about a fire-
man who had brought his truck and a woman who had brought
her ambulance. Her smile was bright as she described to me the
shiny vehicles. I didn't have anything with flashing lights and
loud sirens to impress the children or to help them understand
what I did for a living.

On the day of the visit, my little friend beamed when I pulled
out my purple bag filled with Hershey Kisses. What had been

given to me, I gave to them. I talked about the bag and the special gift that she and her friends had given me. I told them that the biggest part of what I do is let people know that they are cared for and loved. Before I finished, I gave each of them a "kiss" to remind them that they were special and loved.

Ultimately, that is our job in the body of Christ. It is what we do. We care and we love. When you are happy, we should be the ones who celebrate with you. When you are sad, we are the ones who call to help you see and feel God's love. When you are alone, we are the ones who can extend our friendship and support.

That is our job. It is what we do. It is how we fulfill the calling that has been placed upon each of us. Who are the ones around you needing that reminder today? You don't need a fancy truck or a loud siren to remind them. All you need is a "kiss" of love.

Loving God, remind me today that I am loved and that I can love in your name. Amen.

---

5. Nothing but Love

Owe no one anything, except to love one another; for the one who loves another has fulfilled the law.

(Romans 13:8)

Author B. Glenn Wilkerson tells a wonderful story about the power of love. A professor gave his students an assignment. He

71

told them to go to an impoverished area, identify two hundred boys ages twelve to sixteen, investigate their backgrounds and environment, and make a prediction about their future. After conducting interviews and gathering as much information as they could, the students predicted that 90 percent would be incarcerated at some time in their lives.

Twenty-five years later, another group of students was given the assignment of testing that prediction. After getting in touch with 180 of the two hundred boys, they discovered that only four had ever spent time in jail—a surprisingly good record in light of the challenges they faced. The students discovered through their interviews that there was a teacher who had made a difference—and in most cases, it was the same teacher.

The students managed to locate the teacher in a retirement home and asked her how she had made such a remarkable difference in the boys' lives. When they asked if she could give a reason why the boys remembered her, she said no. Then, as she reflected, she said quietly, "I sure did love those boys."[11]

Love makes all the difference. It can turn enemies into colleagues, strangers into friends, and problem children into responsible adults. Love will enable us to see everyone, even the loners, losers, and lost ones of the world, as precious and valued children of God.

As a part of the church, you and I are called to incorporate our love for God into the kinds of actions that will reveal God's love for others in and through us. There is always a choice. But to choose anything less than love will cause discord, chaos, and conflict. In many ways, love is a matter of life or death.

Today, choose love as the driver for all that you say and do.

Loving God, soften my heart with your love so that I may, in turn, love those around me. Amen.

NOTES

1. Joe Bayly, *The View from a Hearse: A Christian View of Death* (Bloomington, IN: Clearnote Press, 2014), 41.

2. King Duncan, "A House Divided," accessed Nov. 7, 2015, https://www.sermons.com/sermon/a-house-divided /1346934.

3. "The Wise Woman's Stone," a widely told moral story of unknown origin.

4. Lewis Timberlake and Marietta Reed, *Born to Win: You Can Turn Your Dreams Into Reality* (Wheaton, IL: Tyndale House, 1986), 123.

5. Vacation Bible School story found at http://climbinghigher .org/lets-make-the-church-together-2/.

6. Lewis Carroll, *Through the Looking Glass* (Mineola, NY: Dover Publications, 1999), 47.

7. Adapted from a story found in Roy B. Zuck, *The Speaker's Quote Book* (Grand Rapids, MI: Kregel, 2009), 223–224.

8. Adapted from a story told by Ernest A. Fitzgerald, *Keeping Pace: Inspirations in the Air* (Greensboro, NC: Pace Communications, Inc., 1988), 163.

9. Gordon MacDonald, *The Life God Blesses: Weathering the Storms of Life That Threaten the Soul* (Nashville, TN: Thomas Nelson Publishers, 1997), 183.

10. Adapted from "Babe Ruth—A Little Boy Hugged Him in Disgrace," from *Our Daily Bread*, accessed Nov. 11, 2015, http://www.familytimes.net/illustration/Loyalty/201540/.

11. B. Glenn Wilkerson, *If Jesus Had a Child* (Castle Rock, CO: CrossLink Publishing, 2014), 3–4.

ABOUT THE AUTHOR

Thomas J. Bickerton is a gifted storyteller and wise mentor who happens to be the Bishop of the Western Pennsylvania Annual Conference of The United Methodist Church. He is a native of West Virginia and the chief spokesperson for the denomination's "Imagine NO Malaria" campaign, which is reducing malaria-related death and illness in sub-Saharan Africa. In addition to being an avid sports fan, he enjoys photography, movies, and travel. He and his wife, Sally, have four grown children.